NEW YORK
AS A
SECOND
LANGUAGE

D0645040

Other Books by Molly Katz

Jewish as a Second Language

Nobody Believes Me

Love, Honour, and Kill

No One Saw Anything

Presumed Guilty

NEW YORK

AS A

SECOND LANGUAGE

★ HADDABEA NEYAWKA ★

MOLLY KATZ

**Andrews McMeel
Publishing**

Kansas City

New York as a Second Language © 2004 by Molly Katz. All rights reserved. Printed in the United States of America. No part of this book may be used or reproduced in any manner whatsoever without written permission except in the case of reprints in the context of reviews. For information, write Andrews McMeel Publishing, an Andrews McMeel Universal company, 4520 Main Street, Kansas City, Missouri 64111.

04 05 06 07 08 MLT 10 9 8 7 6 5 4 3 2 1

ISBN: 0-7407-4189-6

Library of Congress Control Number: 2003114756

Book design by Holly Camerlinck
Illustrations by Kevin Brimmer

Attention: Schools and Businesses
Andrews McMeel books are available at quantity discounts with bulk purchase for educational, business, or sales promotional use. For information, please write to: Special Sales Department, Andrews McMeel Publishing, 4520 Main Street, Kansas City, Missouri 64111.

To my grandma, Mollie Goldenberg Chuckrow (1892–1975), the quintessential Neyawka—who, among many outrageous services to humankind, stood nightly on the roof of her One University Place apartment building in her Air Raid Warden helmet in 1952 watching for enemy planes. Sometimes I think she's still there.

CONTENTS

ACKNOWLEDGMENTS

For the contributions and the laughs, thanks to:
Henry Morrison
Bill Parkhurst
Steve Simon
Sherry Koski
Tom Koski
Deborah Scire
Paul Marcarelli
Cynnamyn
Dickie Akin
William T.
The regulars at Harbor Lights and
the Grand Central Oyster Baw

NEW YORK
AS A
SECOND
LANGUAGE

INTRODUCTION

I've just spent three months introducing my cousin Boodie to life in Neyawk. I helped her move here from Catfish Crossing, Tennessee. Boodie had a mission: to leave her old life behind and make a new one here. She's wanted to be a Neyawka all her life. She planned to get a job, find a place, meet new people. She needed my help.

This has not been easy. Boodie is a quick learner, but avoiding the back wheels of a garbage truck isn't the same as acing your math final. Confusing the multiplier with the multiplicand doesn't result in death.

But I promised I'd teach her everything she'd need, and that became *my* mission. I love my cousin. And I love my city.

I drew up a lesson plan. I created exercises and notes for Boodie to study. I took her into the field every day and never left her side. I couldn't, because she'd be unsafe until she understood our psychology. Why we do what we do.

See, Neyawkas never have enough room. Our living spaces are tiny, our streets can't fit one more vehicle or our sidewalks one more body. We think we never have enough of *anything*. Thus we must be constantly vigilant. Others try to take what's rightfully ours, which is reprehensible. We try to take what they consider theirs, which is necessary.

Neyawk is about convincing as many people as possible to give up and go away.

These facts make strategies and contests out of life functions that outside of Neyawk are simply life functions.

Picking a flower or parking your car or buying lunch are exactly that in Tuscaloosa. In Neyawk . . . well, that's what Boodie needs me for.

I'm the perfect person to help Boodie, because Omma Neyawka. Awaz bawn heah.

Am I losing you already? Okay. I'm a New Yorker. I was born here. When I was a tiny kid, I'd sit at the window of my grandparents' apartment overlooking Washington Square Park, eating oatmeal that Grandma divided into clumps corresponding to the city. ("Now eat Eighth Street. Now eat the Central Park Zoo.")

I don't whistle through my fingers for a cab (that's only in Meg Ryan movies), but I understand that if I try to cut one off in traffic, I'll lose.

Yes, I drive in Neyawk. There's an art to it. I'll get to that. Be patient (something Neyawkas never are, but think everyone else should be).

You've probably heard a really lot of nasty things about Neyawkas. We're rude. Negative. Opinionated. Hyper.

Aggressive. Competitive. We yell a lot. We don't listen.

These are all true. We just don't see them as nasty things. They're survival skills.

So, listen. If, like Boodie, you're from attatan, or ya gonna be transferred tada city or whateva, ya gotta learn a lotta stuff. Even if you never intend to come here, though, ya gotta deal with Neyawkas everywhere. A Neyawka who's been in Duluth for forty years is still a Neyawka. Part of being one is that we never realize, no matter how long we live someplace else, that other people don't act or tawk like us.

Once you learn our language, you'll start to understand.

Here are all the lessons I taught Boodie. Think of me as your interpreter, your coach, and your spiritual guide. Stick with me, and when we're done . . . yagonnabea Neyawka.

WELCOME TADA CITY

I went down to Catfish Crossing and drove us up to Neyawk. Letting Boodie do that alone would have been like sending her to 127th Street to ask directions to Negro Avenue.

I figured the trip would be a good introduction to some of the lessons I'd planned, and I was right. (Neyawkas always are.)

For instance, the tollbooth at the George Washington ("Geedubya") Bridge that leads from New Jersey into

Neyawk. Boodie watched as I paid the man and drove off.

"He didn't say thank you," she commented.

"Of course not," I said. "Notice anything else?"

"Uh . . . kind of a tension?"

I nodded. "You know how, in Tennessee, people always try to make each other feel comfortable? They chat, they smile, they don't rush you?"

"Sure."

"Here it's the opposite. Like just now when I paid the toll, the guy didn't say hi or thank you, and neither did I. Being cheery is a sign of weakness. Then we played the arm game. He holds his hand just beyond my reach, and I hold the money just beyond his. Neyawk is full of contests like that."

Boodie blinked. "Paying a toll is a contest?"

"Everything is a contest."

Her permanent smile was starting to fade. "There's a lot more to learn than I thought."

"Don't worry," I said. "I wrote everything down. You'll have notes to review."

As we approached my building, I decided on a slight change of plan. I'd intended to park on the street or in the pockin grodge, to get another lesson in. But Boodie was already a little shaky. Those would have to come later.

THE GEOGRAPHY OF NEYAWK

 Safely settled in my apartment, I made us tea and we collapsed on the couch. Actually, *I* collapsed—Boodie sat primly.

"Honey, kick your shoes off," I said. "Relax. Sprawl."

"Why?" she asked, gingerly obeying.

"One of your first lessons. Neyawkas claim turf with their body parts. It's expected. You'll never stand politely at a counter anymore. Even little kids know enough to lean on it with both elbows."

We sipped our tea. I'd had to hunt through my cabinets for an ancient box of Lipton. This wasn't quite the time to teach Boodie about beverage snobbery: that it's not tea, it's Ceylon Hibiscus Beeswax Mango; it's not coffee, but Kenya Rubberplant Mocha. Everything in a New Yorker's life has a pedigree. We must have/be/know/date/be known by/be dumped by/be rejected by the best. "Leo DiCaprio broke up with my masseuse" is as impressive as "We have a standing table at Rao's."

Boodie said, "You know that old cartoon of a New Yorker's view of the world, with all the other places smaller than New York? Is that true?"

"God, no," I said. "Neyawkas don't think there *are* any other places. Except some little bits of Connecticut and New Jersey that are considered New York. Wait—I made you a map."

I pulled out my lesson plan and showed her this:

While she studied it, I looked through the lessons and decided to start tomorrow with an easy introductory topic—how Neyawkas tawk.

MASTERIN THE
NEYAWK ACCENT

The next day dawned warm and smoggy. Boodie hadn't slept well.

"There's so much noise," she said.

"Yes," I said proudly. "It's part of our Neyawk macho. We love to travel to quiet places and then complain that we can't sleep without the fire engines and gunshots."

Boodie opened the window. She breathed in what she assumed was the fresh air. "The sky looks grayish," she observed.

"That's smog. Humidity with dirt added. Come on, let's get dressed. Lots to do. First, we have to start teaching you the language."

I figured the subway would be a good place to start her off with an earful. I bought us Metrocards from one of the two out of eight machines that weren't broken, and we took seats on the Uptown Local. Next to us two dudes were chatting.

Here's the conversation:

"Gotta biginta vu."

"Fawakyna job?"

"Zekyativ job."

"Galuck."

Translation:

"Got a big interview."

"For what kind of job?"

"Executive job."

"Good luck."

Boodie whispered to me, "What language is that?"

"English."

"No," she said.

"Yes. I'll teach you."

Here are the instructions I gave her:

- Work on one sound at a time. Practice using all parts of your mouth at once for each sound. Neyawkas pronounce every word with the help of the tongue, lips, teeth, gums, and whatever happens to be being chewed at the moment.

- To speak in our distinctive jumbled-word sentences, pretend there's a velour-covered golf ball on your tongue, and you have to talk around it.

- Another useful image is to speak as if someone were pushing your words together and gluing them in place as they come out of your mouth.

I made Boodie practice speaking, listening, and interpreting. It was slow work, like teaching a toddler to use a fork. But she had to have the basics if she was going to navigate the verbal swamp of her new city.

TRUE NEYAWK MOMENT #1

A limo is dispatched to a hotel bar to pick up a couple and drive them home to the suburbs. They get into the car, very drunk. They begin kissing and canoodling. Suddenly the man screams.

"What's the matter?" the driver shouts.

The man says, "This isn't my wife!"

GETTIN SETTLED IN NEYAWK

Real Estate

"I love your apartment," Boodie said, looking around at my polished oak floors and cute bay window. "I'm going to get one just like it. Maybe with a big kitchen."

"This is a big kitchen," I said, gesturing at mine, which holds a table for two and even has a window. "A small kitchen isn't a room. It's half a closet with a toy stove and a baby fridge underneath. I dated a guy who had to wash his dishes in the bathroom sink."

She looked at me as if I'd said he washed them in the toilet, before flushing.

"Honest," I said. "But listen—before you can even look, we have to get you a real estate agent. This should be easy, but it's not."

I explained to Boodie that everyone in Neyawk is in a hurry, but real estate agents are in a huge, gigantic hurry. They are terribly busy showing way more expensive apartments than you can afford to people who are far more important than you.

I told Boodie to expect the following:

- Whatever your price range is, you'll be told there is nothing available in it except a minuscule insect-ridden studio that faces a halfway house for convicted sex criminals.
- The exact apartment that would have been perfect for you was just taken minutes ago. There never has been or will be another find like it.
- When you ask about a specific apartment advertised, it's already rented, even if you have the ad in your hand from a paper you just saw unloaded off the truck. If you don't have the ad, there isn't and never was any such place.
- There's no point in trying another real estate agent. They're all swamped and won't even return your call. Your agent just happened to have a rare opening today, due to Kim Cattrall canceling. Otherwise you would have been given an appointment for next spring.

- Should they show you an apartment that has one or two of the nine features you require (such as a closet), you must be prepared to take it on the spot and front four months' rent and an elevator-repair deposit.

- When you finally receive the lease to sign, you must do so immediately, or you forfeit the place. The lease prohibits you from having a dog, cat, ferret, overnight guest, or houseplant. You must give ten months' notice if you are moving. The landlord reserves the right to show the apartment to others at any time in your entire lease. You waive your right to take legal action for any reason ever.

Then I had to teach Boodie these real estate phrases:

"Fynana potmint": what the *New York Times* Sunday classifieds help you do.

"Lookida pock": what you can do if you fynana potmint with a view.

"Soday kangedindeah": the reason for locks.

"Kweetawk?": "Is this open to negotiation?"

"Naybahooda": approximately. ("Kweetawk inna nay-bahooda two tousan?")

Emergency Assistance

In Neyawk you can dial a special emergency number for help with residential crises such as collapsed walls or ceilings, water main breaks, poisonous fumes, furnace explosions, and the like. Of course, there are no actual people answering these calls, nor can you leave a message.

Crime

Boodie and I happened to pass a doorway where two less-than-clean gentlemen who weighed about eighty pounds together were exchanging cash and a powdery substance. Boodie spun to stare.

"Jeez," I said, steering her away. "Don't look."

"But that's a crime! Shouldn't we call the police?"

Someone passing us heard her and laughed. I laughed, too.

I explained to my cousin that Neyawkas ignore any wrongdoing that doesn't involve us at that minute. We step unseeingly over the glass of car break-ins. We cover our ears when an alarm sounds. We pass hookers and drug dealers as if they were lampposts.

"The only people we don't ignore," I said, "are the street crazies."

I told Bood that she should never make eye contact with anyone except insane criminals. Looking right at them is an act of aggression that shows the murderers and rapists not to mess with us. They will then skip us and go on to victimize one of the many who avoid looking at them.

"At least in Neyawk," I said, "our psychopaths don't pretend to be anything else. Nuts from California or St. Louis act like real people. Ours mumble in Wolof, scream in your face, froth and drool, and wear their sneakers on their ears. They let us know who they are. It's only fair."

Meetin and Greetin

In Catfish Crossing, you can't stop at the drugstore for breath mints without getting into conversations with everyone you see. (Breath, by the way, is another New York issue. Recently the Taxi Commission had to require drivers to brush their teeth, *with toothpaste,* before their shifts. I swear this is true.)

One morning Boodie and I walked over to Starbucks for some fieldwork on social topics. It was a little after ten, too late for the morning pogrom. I'd planned that. No point having her panic when we were just getting started on her new life.

A neighbor of mine happened to be exiting the place as we entered. "Wanda," I said, "meet my cousin Boodie. She just moved to the city."

"'Hey, Bood,'" Wanda said.

"What did she call me?" Boodie asked when my friend left.

"'Bood.' One syllable. Neyawkas don't have time to pronounce your full name. I only said hers so as not to confuse you. I usually call her Wan. She calls me Mol. Your doorman, your mail carrier, everyone will do the same. Immediately. Barbara is Babs. Anthony is Ant. Or Tone. You'll never hear your last name or your full first name again."

Inside Starbucks, I gave her a quick tour. "That's the counter where you order. Then the next area is where you mill around and wait. When the person at the counter after that yells out that yours is ready, go over and get it. They don't say your name, just what's in the cup. Remember the rules, because if you forget, no one tells you."

"Really?" Boodie asked. "They can't be that unfriendly."

"They're not," I said. "We just express our friendliness differently. It's a mark of respect that we assume you know how not to get eaten by lions."

"Okay," she said dubiously.

"Now for another big lesson. Talking in public. Neyawkas don't have cheery, upbeat conversations," I explained. "Don't be fooled into thinking you're going to have one just because it opens with a positive-sounding statement. Watch."

I approached the counter. "Nice day," I said to the preteen behind it.

"Yeah, well, only when I gotta work," he answered.

I turned to Boodie. "See?" I whispered.

She frowned. "No."

"Okay, we'll practice."

We collected our drinks and took a table.

"A positive comment has to be answered with a negative," I explained; "a 'Yeah, well' or 'Yeah, but.' Neyawkas can't get caught being happy. That might suggest they have nothing to whine about, which is never the case. Say 'Nice day' to me."

"Nice day."

"Yeah, well, it cudinnabin like this Sattiday. Say it again."

"Nice day."

"Yeah, but tomorra they said rain. Now you try. Nice day."

"Yeah," Boodie said, "but . . ."

I smiled encouragingly.

"But . . . the ozone layer."

"Great!" I shouted. "One more. Nice day."

"Yeah, well . . . um . . . finally."

I gave my student a giant smooch on the cheek.

I also taught Boodie about the word *don't*—the first word of a Neyawka's polite response to a polite question:

"Howzya muthuh?"

"Don't ask."

"Ya gointada dennist?"

"Don't remind me."

"Ya hava good trip?"

"Don't get me started."

Then there were these conversational words and phrases she needed to learn:

"Gidada heah!" ("Is that so?")

"Samatta?" ("Have I said something wrong?")

"Gahed." ("Be my guest.")

"Ol kickya rass." ("I'm afraid I disagree.")

"Hava gaweekin." ("See you Monday.")

"Seeya papuh?" ("May I read your newspaper?" Or, informally, "Gimmeya papuh.")

Kagofa: would be interested in. ("I kagofa some pizza.")

Pradavit: prideful. ("Omma Puerto Rican and pradavit.")

Ongunna: I intend to. ("Ongunna godida bank.")

Eaftuh: later on. ("Ol callya eaftuh.")

Jagetcha: the start of an inquiry. ("Jagetcha mail?")

Awhat: Don't you agree? ("Is this cawfee gobbidge, awhat?")

Gadazit: an introductory phrase used for emphasis. ("Gadazit hot!" or "Gadazit ever gonna stop rainin'?")

"Nome sane?" This is not a real question, and there is no answer. Do not reply, "Yes, I know what you are saying."

Aw:

da eighteenth letterada alphabet

The Neyawk Airports

Boodie had never been on a plane, except to fly from home to somewhere in Alabama even smaller than Catfish Crossing to visit her sister. Her home airport is called Quad Cities. This sounds like a busy, important hub. It's not. The other three cities it serves are Bramblebush, Divinity, and North Frogpenis.

Even at its busiest times, Quad Cities Airport contains fewer passengers than any ladies' room at JFK. Boodie's home airports would now be JFK, LaGuardia, and Nork (Newark). So I had to coach her on several points before she used one. Otherwise she might lapse into her ingrained habits of courtesy and get trampled or killed.

I hailed us a cab and we set out for JFK. Boodie's eyes, wide enough already from the Long Island Expressway, turned to moons as we drove into the convoluted cloverleafs of the airport and she watched the instructive signs whiz past. At our airports, you have to memorize confusing and contradictory information in seconds, while continuing to drive fast enough to satisfy cars behind you, and making decisions about where to turn off now, three ramps from now, and when you leave ("Air Peru, Alitalia, and Aeroflot, Terminal B. International Arrivals, Terminal C. International Departures, Station M. Airport Exit, Third Right After Hangar 2F . . .").

"What would we do if we weren't in a cab?" Boodie asked. "Why do they make it so hard to figure out where to go?"

"Because otherwise it would be easy," I said. "Now, look. Here we are at one of the departure areas. What do you see?"

She gazed at the quintuple-parked vehicles. "Nascar?"

Here's what I taught Boodie on this field trip:

- The drop-off areas of our airports are packed with vehicles, but don't let this intimidate you. You have as much right to obstruct traffic as anyone else. Take your time unloading your baggage and stacking it just the way you like. Ignore any uniformed idiots who scream at you to move on.

- Do whatever is necessary to avoid checking a bag. This time waster is not for Neyawkas. It's your urban birthright to zip into a cab upon your return without bothering to wait by a carousel. With practice, you will learn to pack everything you need into a series of awkward, heavy, bulbous carry-on bags that will irritate your flight attendants as well as injure and inconvenience your fellow passengers both onboard your flight and in the airports.

- When you must check a bag, make sure the desk agent understands how important it is for your bag not to get lost. Describe the valuable stuff in it. Share horror stories of the times you and your friends have had suitcases misrouted, and you had to wear the same bra for four days.

■ At the check-in gate, be thoroughly sure your onboard needs are taken care of before you give up your place in line. Question the agent about the safest parts of the plane when choosing your seat. Make certain they'll have Sprite instead of just 7-Up.

- When boarding time arrives, stand and jam the gate area with your carry-ons until your row is called, being sure to block passengers who are boarding, now that they've just finished doing what you're doing. In the jetway, barrel past baby strollers and old folks who have the gall to slow you down.

- At your row, block the aisle as you take your time arranging your stuff. Smash your baggage into the overhead bins. Snap at anyone who tries to smash theirs over yours. Take off your jacket and fold it. Smooth your hair. Unwrap your newspaper and your lunch. Now sit down, hogging as much of the next seat and armrest as you can.

- When claiming your checked bags on your return to Neyawk, hurry to be among the first at the moving carousel. Choose the part closest to where the bags come out—where everyone else is. Position yourself, your carry-on, coats, children, and cart so as to block as big a stretch of the belt as possible from other passengers. Don't let anyone push in front of your fort. Otherwise your bag could go by, and you'd have to wait a whole two minutes for another shot at it.

Da Supamocket

Our supamockets are very small. They only carry very small sizes of everything. This is because our groceries have to fit in our very small kitchens. If you want a large size, you have to go attatan.

Specialty Shops

These abound in Neyawk. They are extremely special-
ized. An Ethiopian-incense store will have only that
incense, and nothing else Ethiopian. Handmade Trappist
monk slippers . . . well, you get the idea. If you go into a
specialty shop, be prepared to pretend you understand
what the folks in there are talking about. Bring money.

**Neyawkas don't trust anything
that they don't have to stand on a long,
inconvenient line to get.**

WHAT TA DO FA ENTERTAINMENT

Goin tada Movies

Boodie loves movies. In Catfish Crossing she'd hit the multiplex every weekend. But movie theatas in Neyawk are a whole different experience. On any given evening, there are far more would-be moviegoers in New York than movie theater seats. That's part of the challenge for us. If the film is a new one that the *New York Times* liked, this applies to all times of the day. Weekend evenings are for advanced masochists only.

Here's what I'm teaching her:

- Neyawkas can't enjoy a movie they don't have to suffer to see. Pick your film by how long the line is. If you have to stand outside for hours in sleet to buy a ticket that gives you the right to stand on another line, so much the better.

- The smaller the theater, the harder you should try to get in there.

- Nothing gives Neyawkas more satisfaction than cutting in on a line. Any line, but movies are irresistible to us. We'll concoct any excuse—"I'm buying these for Matthew and Sarah Jessica's nanny." Keep an eagle eye out for such slimebuckets. Loudly confront them. If you cut in yourself, have disgusting overreactive insults ready for the stick-up-the-asses who confront *you*.

- Once inside, save a row of seats for friends who might be joining you. Bring a few extra sweaters to drape over these, indicating that they're taken.

The garments are the signal to people looking for seats that they are invited to demand that you give them up. If you can't find any to save, argue with people who *are* saving.

- Nobody expects you to watch the movie quietly. Groan, scream, or shout at appropriate moments in the action. Showcase your film knowledge by announcing the names of the actors as they appear. Muse aloud about what you think is going to happen. Explain the jokes.

Huh fuh:

what a woman wears tada movies when it's cold out

Sportin Events

Neyawk has numerous stadiums and other facilities where, theoretically, one can watch baseball, football, hockey, basketball, and seasonal treats like tennis or golf tournaments.

When attempting to take advantage of these venues, though, we can't

- move in the traffic
- get in
- pock
- move in the crowd once in
- see anything
- get out
- drive once out

The way to enjoy a sportin event is to go to LaGuardia and fly to a city that actually wants you to have a good time there.

Baw:

where ta go eaftah da game ta getta coupla brooz

Eatin Out

Going to restaurants is our favorite thing to do, next to jaywalking. Neyawk has so many restaurants that if the entire city went to dinner on the same night, there would still be vacant tables. Naturally, we all want to go to the same places. If everyone isn't scheming, lying, and fighting to eat there, it can't be any good.

GENERAL DINING RULES

- When reserving, make up a 212 phone number for yourself. Manhattan restaurants have no respect for 516, 718, 914, 203, or, God forbid, 201.

- Forget about dining on Saturdays between 7:30 and 9:00 P.M. There are no such reservations available ever.

- Upon entering the restaurant, you need time to scope out the place. Stop dead in your tracks and look around for a while, no matter how many people are behind you trying to get in.

- Don't trust the host to find your reservation. Push behind the desk, peer at the book, and point it out.

- Watch with your eagle eye to make sure no one who came in after you is seated first. Should this criminal act occur, pounce on the host and demand an explanation.

- Feel free to show up with five more people than you reserved for. If a restaurant can't be flexible, they shouldn't be in business.

- In the winter, only go to restaurants that have a fireplace. Insist on sitting by it. Complain that you're hot.

- In the summer, only go to restaurants that have sidewalk tables. Insist on sitting out there. Complain that the sun's in your eyes.

- Ask for the waitperson's recommendations and then reject them.

- Never order a dish without asking at least four unanswerable questions about it. ("Is it very salty?" "Is it a big enough portion?" "How many fat grams does it have?" "Can they make it with flaxseed oil?")

ETHNIC RESTAURANTS

We Neyawkas pride ourselves on our knowledge of other cultures. We refuse to think there might be limits to our sophistication or that there's something we don't know everything about. We can't ever be the learner or the impressee.

- We truly believe that Cambodian or Bangladeshi restaurant employees love to hear us stumble around in their language. We're insulted if our attempts are received with anything less than delighted understanding (even if we just said, "May Allah swallow your necktie" when we thought we were ordering fish sauce).

- If we know one Laotian (or Slovakian, or Burmese) person anywhere in the world, we're shocked if they don't know him, too.

- We know these efforts will have the restaurant folks believing that we have dined often in their native land, and they will thus be overwhelmed by our worldliness and treat us as their honored friends.

What to do in an ethnic restaurant

- If the place is Asian, be outraged if there are forks on the table. Demand chopsticks. These should be really weak and splintery, not those paper-wrapped or plastic ones for the tourists. Be sure the staff notices your expert technique with them. Tell your dining companions how often you've been complimented by native Asians.

- If you've been to Budapest or Quito or whatever their city is, share with them the secret spots you discovered there. Tell them they should visit those.

- If you haven't been, discuss with them the special dishes and ingredients of whatever arcane cuisine you do know. Insist they try it.

CHINATOWN

Chinatown restaurants are Neyawkas' idea of the Third World. Thus the staff can get away with alternately ignoring and bullying you. The servers' grasp of English disappears the moment you ask for anything other than what they want to bring you. This is what Neyawkas go there for. We wouldn't trust any other treatment. We're disappointed if we don't get a bad table, bad service, and bad food. The restaurant owners know that just as there are billions of people in China, as many Neyawkas will line up to replace any lost customers. "You don't like it?" they ask rhetorically in Hunanese. "Too bad."

TRUE NEYAWK MOMENT #2

A beggar is sprawled on the sidewalk. His legs are contorted at torturous angles. In front of him there's a cup, and a shakily lettered sign that says CRIPPLED VIETNAM VETERAN—PLEASE GIVE. People drop cash in the cup all day. At 4:30, he stands up, walks to the subway, and goes home.

PITNICKS

Neyawkas adore pitnicking. Boodie thought this meant what it means in Catfish Crossing: packing egg salad sandwiches and enjoying them by a mountain stream.

I explained that her method isn't nearly enough trouble for us. Here's what I taught her:

- Go to Abercrombie & Fitch and get a kidskin pitnick case that contains china plates, silverware, a wine cooler, and stemmed glasses.

- Go to Sherry-Lehmann and choose a wine.
- Go to Bloomingdale's and buy a fringed blanket.
- Go to an enormous gourmet store, like Zabar's. Spend a couple of hours selecting oily, garlicky, wet, dripping prepared foods, like olive and anchovy salad, or duck ravioli with artichoke vinaigrette.
- Find a scrap of grass somewhere.
- Lay out your blanket to cover the broken glass, cigar stubs, pigeon droppings, used condoms, and crack vials. Take off your shoes and socks. Stretch out luxuriantly.
- Unpack your meal. Ignore the folks next to you with three teeth talking to Jesus. Enjoy.

Contests

When I brought this up with Boodie, she thought I meant bake-offs (having once won a $100 savings bond and a lifetime supply of Sani-Flush for her Lemon Peanut Fritters). I explained that there are several types of friendly competitions we Neyawkas enjoy:

CROSSING THE STREET

Contest A: As soon as the DON'T WALK sign flashes, head for the opposite curb, maintaining a confident, unhurried pace. Look straight ahead, being careful not turn at the sound of profanity, horns, screams, sirens, or a death rattle.

Contest B: Upon spotting a crosser from your car, accelerate toward him or her. Victory is achieved if you make the person look; extra credit if they hustle to get out of your way.

COMMUTER TRAINS

Another sport takes place on commuter trains. "But are people still New Yorkers if they live in the suburbs?" Boodie asked as we walked through Grand Central Station.

"Of course. Remember your map. Commuters don't sleep in the city, but having to participate in commuter-train gladiator events more than makes up for that. Come on. I'll show you on the train."

These were today's exercises:

Copping the train seat

Contest A: Take an empty double seat on a peak-time commuter train. Spread your body parts around as far as possible. Pile your belongings next to you. Include something wet without a lid. Glare at anyone who seems about to ask if the seat is taken. A win is achieved if no one sits down.

Contest B: Walk through the train car, ostentatiously seeking a seat. Locate the commuter who's gone to the most trouble to protect his. Extra credit if he's just started

eating something. Say "Excuse me!" Wait patiently while
he moves his possessions. Congratulations.

Irritating other passengers

- Fall asleep. Drool. Snore.
- Listen to music on headphones. Keep the volume
  high enough so that others hear an insistent loud
  buzz.
- Work on your laptop. Let it make a territorial state-
  ment for you as the corners jab your seatmates.
- Converse at the top of your lungs with a colleague.
  The more boring your job, the better.
- Eat something that smells really disgusting.

Entering the subway car

Neyawkas know exactly where to stand on the platform
so as to cluster at the doors of the arriving train. Push in
before anyone can get off. Extra points if you bulldoze
any exiting passengers so far back inside that they miss
their stop.

Then there are numerous verbal competitions. "These are tougher," I told Boodie, "because the player has to think ahead and talk authoritatively at the same time."

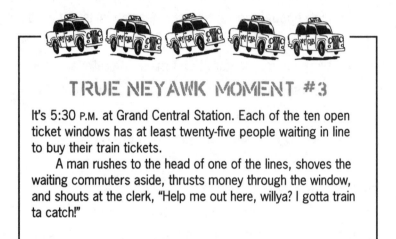

TRUE NEYAWK MOMENT #3

It's 5:30 P.M. at Grand Central Station. Each of the ten open ticket windows has at least twenty-five people waiting in line to buy their train tickets.

A man rushes to the head of one of the lines, shoves the waiting commuters aside, thrusts money through the window, and shouts at the clerk, "Help me out here, willya? I gotta train ta catch!"

ASSIGNING FAULT (ALSO CALLED: "WUDINNA")

This contest consists of the race to make whatever happened, is happening, or is going to happen, someone else's fault.

Boodie and I were in my apartment, waiting for a plumber to finish curing my leaking shower faucets. I've fixed them before on my own, but I was pretty sure I could get a live demonstration of fault passing from this guy.

"Watch," I whispered to Boodie as he wrote up his bill.

He handed it to me. $189.00. I gasped. But it was worth the price when he said . . .

"This wudinna cost so much to fix if you wudinna tried doin it yaself."

I gave Boodie a couple more examples:

"I wudinna been late if ya wudinna gave me the wrong directions."

"She wudinna got pregnant if the condom wudinna broke."

"I wudinna divorced her if she wudinna hada goda Bingo every night."

The all-purpose fault-assigning response to anything anyone asks you: "You tell *me*."

Arguing Over Directions

Neyawkas can't find Guam on a map, but we enthusiastically spend hours debating the best way to get from TriBeCa to Central Park West. Of course, there is no best way.

Vacationing

"I'd love to take a weekend and go to a beach," Boodie said one day after a particularly exhausting lesson at a deli counter, where she had to learn to pronounce seven types of salami. "Let's relax."

"We can go to the beach," I said. "But it won't be relaxing."

I gave her this rundown on our choices:

Fire Island

The quintessential Neyawk vacation spot. It is tiny, crowded, inconvenient, and expensive. It can only be reached by crowded ferry (if you can find space in the crowded parking area of the terminal for your car). It also boasts these coveted features:

- Restaurants (not enough) that are even more packed, have even more inflated prices, and even more indifferent service than in da city.

- A few tiny stores that don't carry anything you need and charge $6.99 for a quart of orange juice. You can either patronize these or lug bags of groceries on the boat. We Neyawkas like doing both.
- You have to walk everywhere, on wee streets that have no logic. Or you can take a water taxi. A water taxi is the only thing worse than a taxi.
- It's full of whining, shoving, bitching Neyawkas.

The Hamptons and the Jersey Shore ("Downashaw")
These are just as obnoxious, but at least there are roads in and out of them.

Maine, Massachusetts, and Rhode Island beaches
These are out-of-the-way. We like to go there and then complain that they're out-of-the-way.

Pitchiz:
whatcha take witcha camera

WORKIN IN NEYAWK

Before moving to Neyawk, Boodie worked as a cosmetologist. In Catfish Crossing, this means selling blue eyeshadow and lipstick the color of Haley's M-O at a Rite Aid. So naturally she was excited about trying another type of job.

Boodie was on the couch, going through the *Times* classifieds. She hadn't quite managed the New York slump/sprawl yet, but at least she no longer sat upright with her feet crossed at the ankles.

"So many openings!" she said. "Salesperson.

Waitress. I have experience at those. I could be a ticket seller in a theater. Here's an ad where they train you to be a computer repair person. These all sound good. What do you think?"

"Well," I said, "they're probably fine. Just be prepared for the differences from home."

Here's what I taught her about how to do these jobs.

Sales Clerk

- Be busy talking to another salesperson as a customer approaches. Let the customer wait while you finish your chat.
- That done, now is the time to be in a hurry. Make sure the customer understands how many more important tasks you have to do than sell her something.
- If you must show her an item, gaze at the chandelier and drum your fingers on the counter while she considers it.

- Be careful to leave the price tags off the most desirable items. Make the customer ask how much they are. Answer condescendingly.
- If the customer requests an item not on display, rummage through every drawer and cabinet to find it. Show her the biggest, glitziest, priciest size of whatever it is. Tell her it's a limited edition.
- If you can't find what she's asking for, say you have to look in the back*. Take forever. Return without it.
- Rush through the paying transaction as fast as possible so you can go on to not helping the next person.

* In the back: A magic place that contains all the merchandise in the world except the item the customer wants.

Restaurant Work

FAST FOOD

- Demand the customer's order as he or she is approaching the counter. Do this by gazing over the person's shoulder and shouting, "Kelpyu?" (Or, if rushed, "Pyu?") Beware of slowpokes who insist on reading the selections first.

- It is part of your job to repeat the order into your microphone even faster than the customer is saying it.

- Before the customer has finished ordering, scream, *"Next!"*

TRUE NEYAWK MOMENT #4

A woman on line at Kentucky Fried Chicken orders three large buckets of wings.

Clerk: "For here or to go?"

Woman: "Do you think I'd eat all this food by myself?"

Clerk: "Bitch, do I know your life?"

COFFEE SHOP/DELI

- Be sure there are different counters and waiting lines for each service (hot food, cold food, drinks, etc.). Don't mark these. Practice keeping a straight face when you send attatanas to the end of another line after they've slowly worked their way to the front of yours.

- Think of all the essentials your customers will request (salt, mustard, forks, etc.). Hide them on some tiny table that's impossible to find. When they ask, gesture meaninglessly and say, "Ovadeah."

- Chew garlic.
- If your shop has tables, sprinkle Coke drips and crumbs on them.
- Greet your regulars by name. Ignore anyone you don't know. When newcomers insist on being served, do so grumpily.

FOINE DOINING

- Let arriving patrons stand around a while before being seated. This sets the correct mood by limiting their expectations.
- If they have a reservation, pretend you can't find it in the book. If they don't, shake your head and cluck. Don't let the fact that you have many empty tables interfere with this formality. Neyawkas are disappointed if you make dining out too easy for them.

- Be icily polite. That's what they're paying so much for. Cheeriness they can get attatan.
- *You* decide the pace of the meal. If customers try to leisurely peruse the menu when it's convenient for you to take their order, hover and loom and tap your pencil.
- Be sure any errors on the check are in your favor. If the customer catches them, make clear your opinion of nitpickers.

Ticket Seller
(Movies, Plays, Museums, Train, Etc.)

- Have a novel open at all times.
- Never make eye contact with customers.
- The thicker your window, the softer you speak.
- Pretend not to hear half of what you're asked.
- See how few words you can waste responding to the other half.

- Be extra rude with tourists. Do you want them to go home and say Neyawk is *friendly*?

Toll Collector/Grocery Cashier

- Leave the light on your lane green after you close it. When the next driver or shopper enters, act like *they're* the idiot.

TRUE NEYAWK MOMENT #5 :

A woman's furnace quits on a Sunday in February at 1:00 A.M. She opens the Yellow Pages to the repair companies that say "Emergency service, call anytime." She dials a number and explains the problem.

The man answering says, "Are you crazy? It's one o'clock in the morning."

Medical Receptionist

- Have your back turned to your window at all times.
- When patients call, remember that your primary responsibility is to not let them speak to the doctor. Feel completely free to dispense complex medical advice.
- Unless they're calling for test results, in which case you can't give out that information.
- Bellow intimate questions at patients across a crowded waiting room: "Mrs. Duncliffe, is your vaginal discharge still green?"

Repair Person

- Don't feel you have to get there on the appointed day. This is merely a guideline.
- Upon viewing the problem, ask incredulously, "Who woiked on this befaw?"

- Be sure not to have with you whatever part is needed. Say without much hope that you might have it in the shop,* otherwise, it will have to be ordered from Khartoum.
- Tell the customer how lucky he is that this didn't happen sooner, or worse, or more expensively than whatever preposterous amount you're going to charge.

Airport Employee

SECURITY GUARD—GATE ENTRANCE

In this role you must make your security decisions very carefully. When searching passengers, you don't want to waste your energy on scruffy, smelly foreign types. Your job is to amuse yourself. Select the most attractive woman (if you're male) or man (if you're female). Have the person

---

* In the shop: Another magic place (see "In the back," p. 59).

remove their shoes and any other pieces of clothing you choose, then strike entertaining poses. When you get bored with him/her, begin scouting for your next subject.

SECURITY GUARD—EXIT

Don't bother checking luggage tags when the airport isn't busy. Instead, wait till three 747s with numerous bearded Iraqis on board have just landed. This is the time to swing into action. Position yourself by the exit and scrutinize each tag of each bag of each passenger. Let your coworkers go do something else—you can handle this yourself. See how long a line you can keep waiting. Take turns competing with your buddies.

General Guidelines on Dealing with the Public

- When answering the phone at your job, hurriedly mumble the firm name. If the caller can understand it, you're not answering correctly.

- Don't be bashful about sharing your personal problems with customers. If you didn't sleep well, or you're constipated, or your supervisor is a pervert, you need to vent.

- As you conclude each transaction, say "Havagaday" or whatever your employer requires—but remember to use a bored, sullen tone, lest patrons think you really are expressing a gracious sentiment or, heaven forbid, thanking them for their business, rather than simply obeying company policy.

It was time to take Boodie to the Painted Parrot, my favorite baw, for happy hour and networking. I had on a black DKNY skirt suit and my Gucci watch. Bood came out of the bathroom in powder blue capris and matching tank. Everything she wears matches.

I shook my head.

Her face fell. "You don't like this?"

"It's adorable. But not for happy hour. You have to look like you just came from work."

"But I didn't."

"All the more reason," I said. "Everyone there is dressed like a CEO. The unemployed folks look the best. How can you expect to get a job if people think you don't have one?"

She changed into pleated pants and a dark green jacket, and we went to the Parrot.

Inside, Boodie headed for a stool.

"Back here," I said, gesturing to the end of the baw. "It's where the regulars go. I'll introduce you."

My friend Cynnamyn, butter-blond and vivacious, was right there on her usual seat. "Bood," I said, "Meet Cyn."

Cyn dimpled and pulled Boodie in for a kiss. My cousin looked startled. I'd forgotten to warn her about baw behavior. All the regulars hug and kiss one another and the staff.

I explained to Cyn how I was acclimating Boodie to the city. She caught on right away. She touched Boodie's sleeve.

"Hon," she said, "wear black. Then people stay out of your way. Any other color, you're invisible."

Here are the other pointers Cyn gave her:

- Every baw has a tight group who have been drinking together at the same place at the same time since before you were born, no matter how spontaneous their fun looks. Don't take a stool in their turf. Don't say a word to them. They don't want to know your name, or where you're from, or see the new Movado you bought on the street.

- The baw is not a library. Don't spread out your newspaper. This takes up valuable inches, which to drinking Neyawkas are priceless.

- Don't ask to run a tab if you've been going there less than ten years.

- The regulars signal for a refill with a gesture like an invisible auction bid. You must learn how to do this. Don't yell, "Hey, Barney, hit me again."

- Don't use an earpiece to talk on your cell phone. You look mentally ill.

- Tip the bathroom attendant. She's not there because she wants to hear you pee. Give her a dollar.
- Tip the bartender 20 percent, no matter how crappy the service was.
- Don't touch the bar snacks. The regulars don't go home and broil a lamb chop. This is their dinner.

Snow

Snow in Neyawk is like snow in Florida. We're always astonished when we get it. It isn't in our lease. Nobody owns a shovel or has snow tires on their car, taxi, or truck.

This is our Disney wonderland. We immediately make hot chocolate and get out our scarves, boots, and mittens. We see nothing at all ridiculous about putting on our cross-country skis and poling our way down Madison Avenue.

Boodie's idea of a state of emergency is a tornado that wrecks homes and kills people. A Neyawk state of emergency is snow on a Tuesday afternoon. Everyone leaves work early. TV news crews film us slipping and sliding on the sidewalks. They'll wait all day for a shot of someone's umbrella blowing inside out or a quote from a plow driver calling the storm the worst he's seen in twenny-two yeahs onna road.

It is not really necessary to pick up after your dog. Simply hold a plastic bag conspicuously in your hand as you walk him.

Meer:

whatcha look in ta comb ya heh

Smoking

Most Neyawkas have long since quit. We are viciously jealous of those who haven't. Thus we feel compelled to make it as tough for them as they do for us. I showed Boodie how to do this:

- When passing within two hundred yards of a smoker on the street, use both arms to ostentatiously wave away the noxious cloud.
- Glare at anyone buying cigarettes. Mumble offensive comments about their life span.
- Fake retching sounds when walking past cigar bars.

- If you catch someone lighting up in one of the countless places they're not supposed to, make an enormous loud commotion about it.

Adjusting Your Personal Timetable

Neyawkas do everything late. We believe nothing important ever happens early. The longest movie line is for the 10:00 P.M. show, even on weekdays.

Only attatanas eat lunch at noon or dinner at 6:00.

On the other hand, I told Boodie, try getting a cheeseburger at 11:00 P.M. in Tulsa.

MOVIN ARANNA CITY

"Bood," I had to keep reminding her, "you're not walking fast enough."

We were on our way to get a sandwich, to nourish ourselves for some driving lessons, and people were passing us on both sides.

"Remember, hon, everything is a contest. You have to always be in a hurry. Watch my posture." I gave her a good look at my walking stance—bent forward, leading with my head. "This helps me move faster and warns everyone else who's in their own hurry that I need to get ahead of them."

Bless her, she did it, arrowing her body like a native, picking up speed like the Roadrunner.

"What if we knock someone over?" Boodie asked.

"That's their problem."

"Or," she said, "it's an opportunity to tell them why it was their fault. 'If y'all wuddina bumped into me . . .' "

Yeah, *baby* . . .

Boodie considers herself a good driver. In Catfish Crossing you're good if you obey signs and signals, are courteous to other drivers, and stick to the speed limit.

When I take Boodie in the car with me in Neyawk, I have to keep checking to see if she's got her eyes closed. She won't learn anything that way.

As she slid nervously into the driver's seat, I reminded her that to us driving is a sport. Anything done behind the wheel is part of the game. She needed to master these principles:

- Treat a YIELD sign as if it says RACE.
- Make sure not to let any interlopers into your lane. As soon as one signals to move over, speed up.
- On entering a highway, immediately get over to the left lane, cutting off as many cars as possible.
- Tailgate the person ahead. Should they have the audacity to not move out of your way, flash your lights, shift from side to side, and generally act like a neurosurgeon rushing to a waiting helicopter. As soon as you succeed in intimidating them

into moving over, repeat the process with the car now ahead.

- Get even with any sonofabitch who tries to do to you what you're doing to everyone else. Catch up to the person, lower your window, and scream one or more of the following:

"Waddaya, drunk?"

"Wherja learnta drive?"

"Ya ratta ya mine!"

Gobbidge trucks:

You may think emergency vehicles are the kings of the road. They're not—these are. They can go in any direction in any lane of any street, and sit in the middle of it all day. They can park as long as they want, wherever they want. The sanitation guys are tenured and overtimed. They make more money than the mayor. They couldn't care less about right-of-way. There is absolutely nothing you can do to hurt them. Their vehicles are indestructible, yours isn't; they know this and they know you know it.

Street Pockin

This is never legal in Neyawk, except above 130th Street. In some other areas, you can pock altnit side. That means you must move your vehicle back and forth from one curb to the other on certain days and at certain hours, so that the street cleaners have room to not clean the streets.

Do not pock illegally. *They will tow your car.* The truck will materialize the instant your time expires, even if a fatal crash just occurred around the corner and no city employees are available to handle that.

They love towing. They will damage your car with the heist. They will lose it in some pound. They don't care. If you wudinna pocked there . . .

The Pockin Grodge

This is a subterranean area where you leave your car for several hours so that the attendants can speed-test your brakes and acceleration and adjust your seat and steering wheel positions, mirrors, and radio station. There is no extra charge for these courtesies.

Boodie is learning to use grodges. She is starting to accept what all Neyawkas know, that there is no way to tell the cost of the grodge until she is so far down the entrance ramp that she can't back out. (The ramp is narrow and twisty for this purpose. Nascar drivers wouldn't attempt it.)

There is a sign outside listing the prices, of course, but it reads something like, "First 10 minutes $4.26. Each extra minute, $12.21. Less than ½ hr., $42.00 minimum. No maximum over 3 hrs. Night rates sometimes apply. Day rates subject to change at night."

I'm also teaching Boodie to interpret the attendants' greetings, questions, and instructions:

"Plova!" ("Leave the car right here, please.")

"Hallong?" ("What time will you be returning?")

"Luckat!" ("Careful, there's another car coming.")

"Yo! Ay!" ("You neglected to leave your key.")

"Wakyna caw?" ("Please describe the vehicle.")

"Waculla?" ("I need a bit more information.")

"Ya dicktwat!" ("You have overlooked the customary gratuity.")

How good has my girl become? Just last Friday, we went to the theater. Her assignment that night was to handle all negotiations.

Of every 300 people seeing a Broadway play, 240 of them are parked in the same grodge as you. They all must have their cars *now*. Neyawkas possess a breathtaking ability to blind themselves to the 239 others standing around who want what they want when they want it.

After-theater, the crack team of fifteen attendants who whizzed your car away the moment you drove in is reduced to two tired guys, one of whom sits in the booth collecting unspeakable amounts of your money between bites of Chinese food.

I was worried.

But Boodie marched us to the front of the line. Only I could feel the tremble in her hand. She stuck the parking stub in the attendant's face. As the couple now behind us opened their mouths to protest, Boodie asked me loudly, *"Are y'all gonna throw up again?"*

They immediately took several steps back.

I was so proud.

Cabs

Neyawk cabdrivers have completed their responsibility once they stop the taxi and permit you to enter it. They are not required to know where they're going or to speak any recognized language. These extras, when available, are complimentary.

Flashing Street Signs

Neyawkas know that the WALK—DON'T WALK indicators are merely a proposal. We wouldn't dream of pushing the button for the WALK sign and expecting it to change anything.

These are there merely to appease attatanas who correctly suspect they have no power in Neyawk.

TRUE NEYAWK MOMENT #6:

It's the Northeast blackout of 2003. A car door opens at a jammed intersection, and the driver jumps out. He hurries into the traffic and halts crossing cars until it clears. Then he runs back to his own car and drives on through.

THINKIN LIKE A NEYAWKA

I'm teaching Boodie that in Neyawk there are only two sides to any issue. She must have a one-dimensional opinion on everything and passionately defend it.

This doesn't mean she has to learn the issues. We compensate for any lack of information simply by expressing our views loudly and angrily. The less well-informed we are, the nastier we get.

Some of Boodie's new vocabulary lessons:

Dayawta.

The phrase used to say what you think should be done.
For example:

Issue: Graffiti artists
Opinion: "Dayawta stickumin jail."

Issue: The homeless
Opinion: "Dayawta truckum tada White House."

Issue: Porn palaces
Opinion: "Dayawta burnum down."

Issue: Potholes
Opinion: "Dayawta fixum."

Issue: Snowy sidewalks
Opinion: "Dayawta shovela mout."

Cudinnabin.

A condition of regret, misfortune, or lost opportunity—
whatever you wanted, you're not getting it, and whatever
you are getting, it isn't what you wanted.

"Ya cuddinabin here two hours ago."

"This sweata cudinnabin here in red."

"I cudinnabin goin away *last* weekend."

Conversations

Neyawk conversations have to be complicated. Any idiot
anywhere else can comment on Britney Spears's hair color.

We don't discuss the weather; we talk about jet
streams and fronts and dewpoints. It doesn't matter that
we have absolutely no idea what these are.

Similarly, we all toss around terms like "prime rate"
and "GNP." This is to show attatanas how very commer-
cially erudite we are here in the hub of finance.

Never give away the fact that you're from attatan. Be quick to adjust your behavior accordingly. Upon getting settled here, be sure you don't:

- Move out of the way of screaming emergency vehicles.
- Walk down the street in a group.
- Fail to lean on your car horn because you believe you will really be fined some hilarious amount.

- Signal your intention to change lanes. You owe nobody this private information.

- Express any problem with paying $300 for a small Christmas tree.

- Hear sirens.

- Admit you've visited the Statue of Liberty or the top of the Empire State Building.

- Refer to Neyawk as anything but "da city."

- See why someone driving in from Boston to have dinner with you doesn't understand why you don't want to go to a restaurant all the way downtown.

- Waste your breath on stupid platitudes like "Excuse me," "Sorry," or "Thanks."

- Admit Central Park isn't "nature."

- Fail to screech your personal business into your cell phone in quiet public places. Your friends need to hear right this minute that you're getting a Brazilian wax or that the pediatrician says your son has strep.

You may have heard that you reveal your attatan status by gazing up at the tall buildings. This is a fallacy. All Neyawkas look upward, watching for falling construction debris, scaffolding, or suicides.

Translating Signs and Spoken English

Certain phrases you're accustomed to hearing or seeing attatan have entirely different meanings in Neyawk.

- "Can I help the next person in line?" (Means, "I'll take the bozo who races over here the fastest.")
- "Walk-ins Welcome" (During a total eclipse of the sun.)
- "All-Day Parking $5.96" (When you enter before 5:00 A.M.)
- "No Job Too Small" (Unless we already have one.)

Christmas Tipping

You must distribute exorbitant tips to everyone who works in or around your building, from the super to the third assistant substitute mail carrier. This is not about Christmas cheer—it's extortion. Your "tip" buys you the minimal services for the next year that the employees are already paid more for than you can earn.

Foreign Neyawkas

I took Boodie into a Korean produce market to buy some strawberries.

We didn't see any.

"Do you have strawberries?" I asked the clerk.

"Looong ha-wa," he said.

"What?" I asked.

"Looooong ha-waaaaa!" he repeated, waving his hands.

We left. Boodie asked me, "What did he say?"

"I have no idea," I told her.

I took this opportunity to explain to Boodie that Neyawk has folks from many countries living and working here. They consider themselves much more genuine Neyawkas than we are. Not that they master our tongue; their Senegalese or Moroccan accents actually thicken, until they have attained the skill of pronouncing English words in no manner you can recognize. The French get Frencher. Brits sound as if they are announcing a polo match.

What they do master is our rudeness, indifference, and haste. So don't waste your time asking them to repeat what they say, or say it slower, or be more polite. They're Neyawkas now; they don't have time.

TRUE NEYAWK MOMENT #7

A panhandler stands up in a full subway car and says, "Ladies and gentlemen, sorry to bother you. You may not believe this, but I come from a nice family. I was taught that it's good manners to bring a gift when you visit someone's home. So, this is my home. Where's my gift?"

Can you pass?

Boodie was excited when someone asked her for subway directions one day.

I agreed that this suggested she was starting to be regarded as a native. But, I said, there are more subtle indications.

You know Neyawkas see you as one of our own when we:

- Don't offer to help you carry something
- Spill coffee or cigarette ashes on you
- Help ourselves to your pickle
- Fail to notice our dog is investigating your crotch
- Step over you when you fall

RAISIN DA KIDS

People back in Catfish Crossing gasp at the idea of raising kids in Neyawk, but Boodie wants to have a family here one day, now that she understands that dirt, danger, crime, and psychosis are essential elements of a healthy upbringing. I've assured my cousin that I'll teach her all she needs . . . starting with language lessons.

Hadda Tawk ta ya Kid

The Neyawk child is raised with a series of phrases that parents who grew up elsewhere must learn.

To summon your child: "Gedova heah!"
To praise: "Gijob!" "Om pradaya!"
To ask how he's feeling: "Wassa*matta*witchoo?"
Other important phrases:

Wherja putcha ("Wherja putcha jacket?")

Gidada ("Gidada bed!")
   ("Gidadada kitchen!")

Jadooya ("Jadooya homewoik?")

Yagadadooda/Yagadagodada
   ("Yagadadooda dishes.")
   ("Yagadagoda school.")
   ("Yagadagoda bed.")
   ("Yagadagodada staw.")
   ("Yagadagodada batroom?")

Yanoddaladda ("Yanoddaladda wear that.")

("Yanoddaladda hitcha bruthuh.")

("Yanoddaladda godida pock.")

Eatin Out with the Kids

Neyawk has lots of child-friendly restaurants where the little ones can sit in a pretend rocket ship or pet a stingray. Of course, these places are for attatannas. *Your* kids are always welcome at *real* restaurants.

- Pick a really stylish, expensive, formal French place. Be appalled if there are no high chairs.

- Encourage each child to order for him or herself. The waitstaff just loves this.
- Have them order anything they feel like trying. Send back what they don't like.
- If the kids get restless, let them run screaming around the dining room and play under other people's tables. Blow off any old poops who object.
- It's the staff's responsibility to keep them safe from hot platters and flaming desserts.
- For a special treat, bring the kids to the baw. Lift them up on the stools. Watch how the bartender gets a kick out of making them complicated frozen virgin drinks while they eat all his cherries and olives.
- A final adorable touch is to let one of the children hand the waitperson their tip.

TRUE NEYAWK MOMENT #8

Two twentysomething guys are apartment hunting. They walk into a building and ask the concierge, "Is there a gym here?"

"No," he says.

"Is there a video rental machine?"

"No."

"How about a pool?"

The concierge says, "You boys don't wannana potmint. You wanna fuckin hotel."

YA READY YET?
DA EXAM

Boodie and I wrote this together. I'm proud to say she was able to make some great contributions.

Compute your score at the end to see if you're ready to call yourself a Neyawka . . .

1. Your Neyawk living room won't contain
    a. shag carpet
    b. more than twelve people
    c. a deer head

2. Someone who cuts you off in traffic should be
   a. ashamed
   b. ignored
   c. killed

3. Our perms are never done by
   a. Sassoon
   b. Fekkai
   c. Toni

4. Neyawkas "Just Say No" to
   a. smoking
   b. drugs
   c. everything

5. We never get our pets
   a. shampooed
   b. vaccinated
   c. free

6. You can get stabbed for
   a. crashing into someone's car
   b. snatching a purse
   c. saying "The Big Apple"

7. Our apartment doors often have
   a. a welcome sign
   b. a friendship wreath
   c. crime scene tape

8. Your idea of personal space is
   a. your own office
   b. a whole subway seat
   c. no one actually standing on your toes

9. To find a pockin spot on the street, Neyawkas are trained to detect someone who is
   a. unlocking his car
   b. leaving a space
   c. thinking about taking his keys out of his pocket

10. Your potmint building has
    a. a doorman
    b. a gym
    c. a larger population than many cities in Uruguay

11. Our shoes never have
    a. scuffs
    b. rubber soles
    c. clip-on bows

12. On most of our sidewalks you'll see
    a. gobbidge
    b. dog poop
    c. chalk outlines

13. Neyawkas are careful to supply their children
    with enough
    a. toys
    b. school supplies
    c. Mace

14. Neyawk men never say
    a. die
    b. prayers
    c. "I like women with meat on them."

15. In a medical office, you're never told
    a. your charges
    b. your diagnosis
    c. "The doctor is waiting for you."

16. Neyawkas trust
    a. their instincts
    b. their bankers
    c. absolutely nobody

17. No Neyawka in history has ever owned
    a. a snowblower
    b. mother-daughter dresses
    c. a timeshare

18. Neyawkas compete over how often we've been
    a. kissed
    b. fired
    c. burglarized

19. Every active Neyawka must carry
    a. insurance
    b. a weapon
    c. a bottle of brand-name water

20. Someone who commits suicide by jumping in front of a commuter train is
    a. desperate
    b. hopeless
    c. inconsiderate

21. You'll never see a Neyawka with a bumper sticker that says
    a. "I brake for no reason."
    b. "My other car is a broom."
    c. "I ❤ NY."

TRUE/FALSE:

1. We all really clean up after our dogs.

2. Your policeman is your friend.

3. When we want fresh seafood, we rush to Red Lobster.

4. A great place to meet new people is the Port Authority Bus Terminal.

5. Yeah, we can't believe it's not butter.

6. There are bargains galore at going-out-of-business sales. Hurry and take advantage before the store closes.

7.   African-Americans love discussing the O. J. case with you.

8.   The young gentlemen eager to clean your windshield at certain intersections are merely goodwill ambassadors who expect nothing in return.

9.   We, too, treat our gay friends as pets.

10.   Yes, those are real $20 bills on the sidewalk, not ads for phone sex.

11.   Your waitperson is delighted to give your party of seven separate checks.

12.   Of *course* those are genuine Kate Spade handbags the street vendors are selling.

13. Cabbies are just kidding with those signs that say, "Don't smoke—driver allergic."

14. Uh-huh, we, too, wait politely in cab lines of fifty or sixty people with our luggage.

15. We can't wait to hear what you think about the homeless.

Scoring

Take 1 point for each *a* answer, 2 for each *b*, 3 for each *c*. Take 0 for each True, 3 for each False.

21 to 49: Jeez! You know, they really miss you in Battle Creek.

50 to 80: Gettin there. Throw away those cute kitchen signs and scatter some soot.

81 to 108: You must have been Fiorello LaGuardia in another life. Welcome! Hava sean'widge! Getcha potmint! Meetcha naybas! Gid*ada*heah!